I0824235

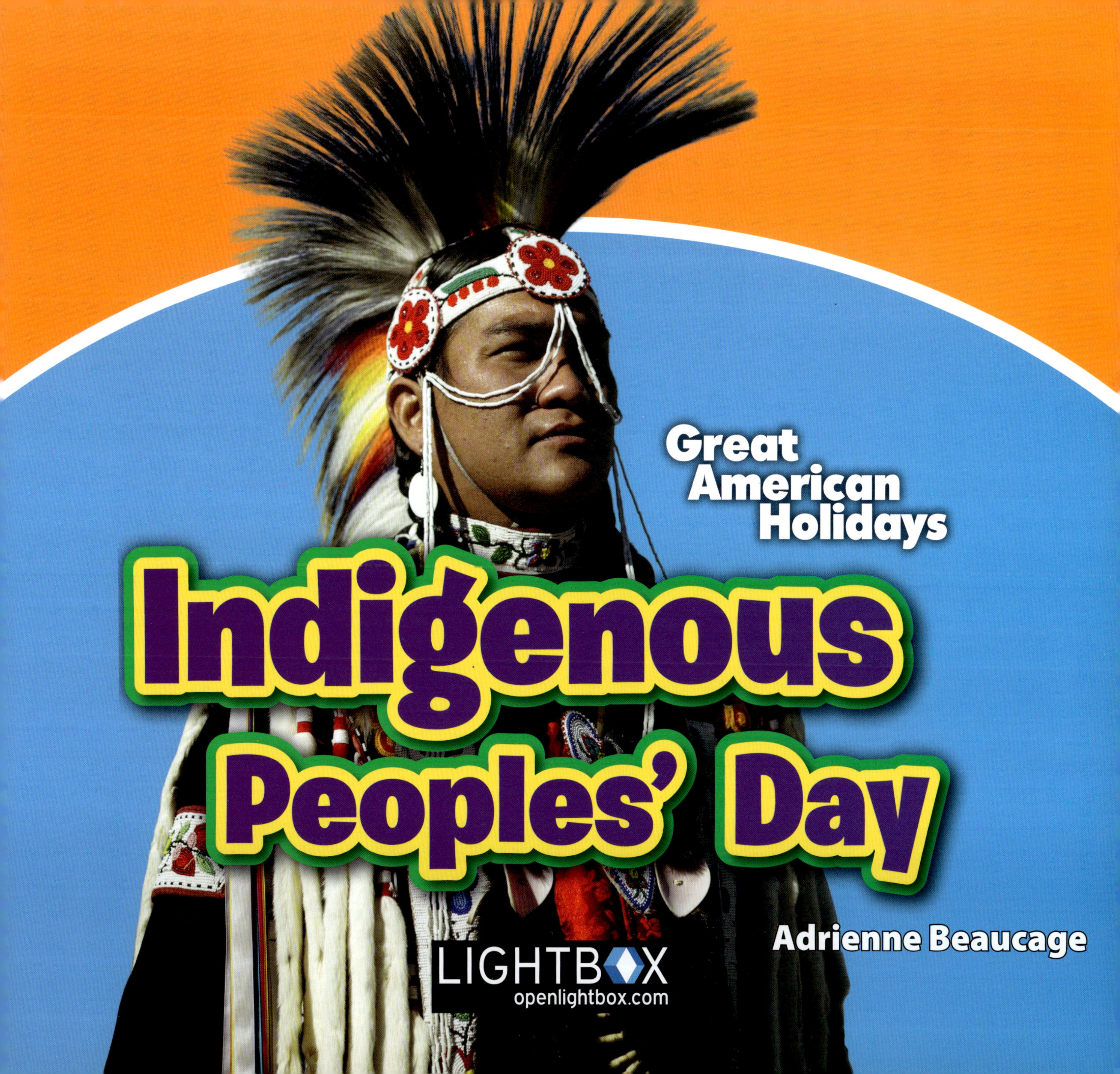
Great American Holidays
Indigenous Peoples' Day
Adrienne Beaucage
LIGHTBOX
openlightbox.com

LIGHTBOX

Go to
www.openlightbox.com
and enter this book's
unique code.

ACCESS CODE

LBXN3827

Lightbox is an all-inclusive digital solution for the teaching and learning of curriculum topics in an original, groundbreaking way. Lightbox is based on National Curriculum Standards.

OPTIMIZED FOR

- ✓ TABLETS
- ✓ SMART BOARDS
- ✓ COMPUTERS
- ✓ AND MUCH MORE!

STANDARD FEATURES OF LIGHTBOX

- **AUDIO** High-quality narration using text-to-speech system
- **VIDEOS** Embedded high-definition video clips
- **ACTIVITIES** Printable PDFs that can be emailed and graded
- **WEBLINKS** Curated links to external, child-safe resources
- **SLIDESHOWS** Pictorial overviews of key concepts
- **INTERACTIVE MAPS** Interactive maps and aerial satellite imagery
- **QUIZZES** Ten multiple choice questions that are automatically graded and emailed for teacher assessment
- **KEY WORDS** Matching key concepts to their definitions

SUPPLEMENTARY RESOURCES

- **SHARE** Share titles within your Learning Management System (LMS) or Library Circulation System
- **CURRICULUM** Find national and state curriculum correlations
- **CITATION** Create bibliographical references following APA, CMSO, and MLA styles

VIDEOS

WEBLINKS

SLIDESHOWS

QUIZZES

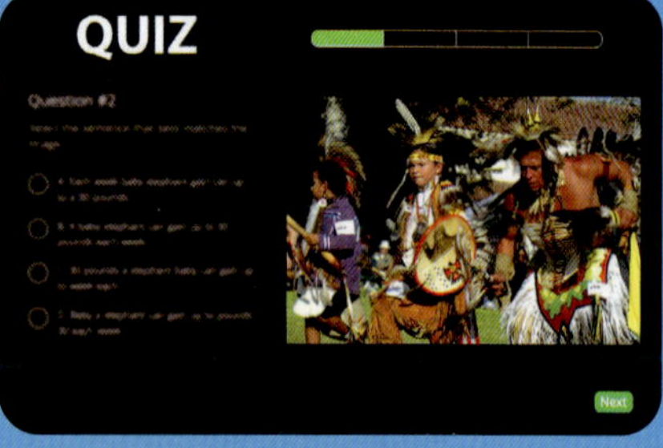

This title is part of our Lightbox digital subscription

Lightbox Grades K–2 Subscription

ISBN 978-1-5105-5423-8

Access hundreds of Lightbox titles with our digital subscription.
Sign up for a **FREE** subscription trial at **www.openlightbox.com/trial**

Great American Holidays

Indigenous Peoples' Day

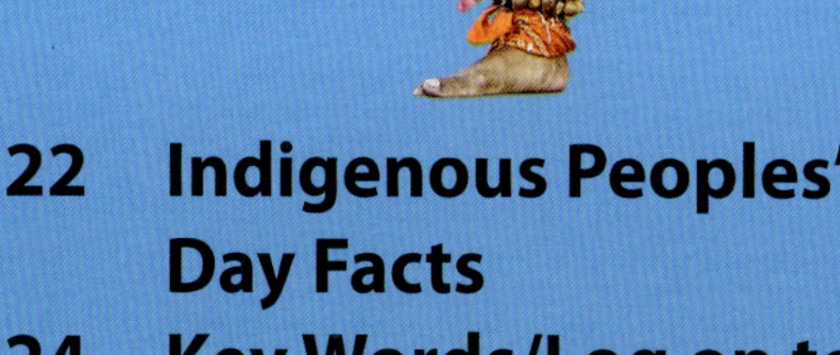

CONTENTS

4

Some people celebrate Indigenous Peoples' Day with parades. Others hold marches to support Indigenous rights.

For many people, Indigenous Peoples' Day is a time to learn about Native American culture. Museums may hold educational events on this day.

INDIGENOUS
PEOPLES DAY
2019
INDIGENOUS
PEOPLES DAY
2019
Port Madison
INDIGENOUS
PEOPLES' DAY

PHILADELPHIA
PARKS &
RECREATION

Stories can help people learn about Indigenous cultures. Some people choose to read books or listen to stories told by Native Americans to celebrate Indigenous Peoples' Day.

INDIGENOUS PEOPLES' DAY FACTS

These pages provide more detail about the interesting facts found in the book. They are intended to be used by adults as a learning support to help young readers round out their knowledge of each holiday featured in the *Great American Holidays* series.

Pages 4–5

Indigenous Peoples' Day is a holiday to honor Native Americans. It is celebrated on the second Monday of October each year.

There are more than 500 recognized Native American nations in the United States.

4 5

Indigenous Peoples' Day is a holiday to honor Native Americans. It is celebrated every year on the second Monday of October. The holiday has been adopted in certain states, cities, and at some institutions instead of or alongside Columbus Day.

Pages 6–7

Indigenous Peoples' Day recognizes that Native Americans were the first people to live in the United States. The holiday honors their history and culture.

Indigenous Peoples lived in what is now the United States thousands of years before people from Europe arrived.

6 7

Indigenous Peoples' Day recognizes that Native Americans were the first people to live in the United States. The day also encourages Americans to consider the darker significance of Columbus Day, which marked the beginning of colonial takeover and violent exploitation of Indigenous people.

Pages 8–9

People first had the idea for Indigenous Peoples' Day in 1977. The first U.S. city to celebrate the day was Berkeley, California, in 1992.

In 2022, Berkeley celebrated the 30th anniversary of Indigenous Peoples' Day.

8 9

People first had the idea for Indigenous Peoples' Day in 1977. The idea for Indigenous Peoples' Day began in 1977, during a United Nations conference. In 1989, South Dakota changed Columbus Day to another holiday, called Native Americans' Day, with its first celebration taking place the following year. In 1992, Berkeley, California, declared it would celebrate Indigenous Peoples' Day instead of Columbus Day. Other cities, and eventually states, would follow suit.

Pages 10–11

Today Indigenous Peoples' Day is celebrated in many places across the United States. More places celebrate it each year.

In 2021, more than 190 cities celebrated Indigenous Peoples' Day.

10 11

Indigenous Peoples' Day is celebrated in many places across the United States. By 2020, more than a dozen states observed Native American or Indigenous Peoples' Day. The holiday is also observed in the District of Columbia. California and Tennessee celebrate Native American Day in late September.

Pages 12–13

Indigenous Peoples' Day is important to Native Americans. All Americans are invited to celebrate the holiday by focusing on Indigenous populations' voices and perspectives, and celebrating their achievements and contributions.

Pages 14–15

There are many ways to celebrate Indigenous Peoples' Day. As a relatively new holiday, specific customs and traditions are still being established. In some cities, celebrations include dancing, songs, and food from local Native American groups, while others incorporate land acknowledgements or film festivals.

Pages 16–17

Some people celebrate Indigenous Peoples' Day with parades. Some places celebrate the holiday with parades. In certain cities, marches are organized to show support for Indigenous Peoples' Day or to denounce the celebration of Columbus Day

Pages 18–19

For many people, Indigenous Peoples' Day is a time to learn about Native American culture. Particularly for non-Indigenous Americans, the day presents an opportunity to learn about Native history, culture, and perspectives. Many museums host special educational events to support Indigenous Peoples' Day. Students and adults are encouraged to learn about historic and contemporary contributions made by Indigenous Peoples.

Pages 20–21

Stories can help people learn about Indigenous cultures. Reading books by Indigenous authors is a way to both raise and celebrate the voices of Indigenous people. Many libraries curate lists of recommended books for Indigenous Peoples' Day. Often, events on Indigenous Peoples' Day feature speakers. The process of passing down history and culture through the spoken word is important to many Indigenous groups.

KEY WORDS

Research has shown that as much as 65 percent of all written material published in English is made up of 300 words. These 300 words cannot be taught using pictures or learned by sounding them out. They must be recognized by sight. This book contains 61 common sight words to help young readers improve their reading fluency and comprehension. This book also teaches young readers several important content words, such as proper nouns. These words are paired with pictures to aid in learning and improve understanding.

Page	Sight Words First Appearance
5	a, Americans, are, day, each, in, is, it, more, of, on, peoples, second, states, than, the, there, to, year
6	and, before, first, from, live, now, that, their, were, what
9	city, for, had, idea, was
10	many, places
13	all, can, important
14	animals, as, food, groups, have, some, such, use, ways
17	others, rights, with
18	about, learn, may, this, time
21	books, by, help, or, read

Page	Content Words First Appearance
5	holiday, Indigenous Peoples' Day, Monday, nations, Native Americans, October, United States
6	culture, Europe, history
9	anniversary, Berkeley, California
14	dancers, dancing, hoops, shapes, songs
17	marches, parades
18	events, museums
21	stories

Published by Lightbox Learning Inc.
276 5th Avenue, Suite 704 #917
New York, NY 10001
Website: www.openlightbox.com

Library of Congress Control Number: 2022944369

ISBN 978-1-5105-5872-4 (hardcover)
ISBN 978-1-5105-5873-1 (multi-user eBook)

Printed in Guangzhou, China
1 2 3 4 5 6 7 8 9 0 22 21 20 19 18

112022
110821

Art Director: Terry Paulhus

Every reasonable effort has been made to trace ownership and to obtain permission to reprint copyright material. The publisher would be pleased to have any errors or omissions brought to its attention so that they may be corrected in subsequent printings.

The publisher acknowledges Getty Images, Alamy, and Wikimedia as its primary image suppliers for this title.